Dear Parent:
Your child's love of reading starts here!

Every child learns to read in a different way and at his or her own speed. Some go back and forth between reading levels and read favorite books again and again. Others read through each level in order. You can help your young reader Improve and become more confident by encouraging his or her own interests and abilities. From books your child reads with you to the first books he or she reads alone, there are I Can Read Books for every stage of reading:

SHARED READING
Basic language, word repetition, and whimsical illustrations, ideal for sharing with your emergent reader

BEGINNING READING
Short sentences, familiar words, and simple concepts for children eager to read on their own

READING WITH HELP
Engaging stories, longer sentences, and language play for developing readers

READING ALONE
Complex plots, challenging vocabulary, and high-interest topics for the independent reader

ADVANCED READING
Short paragraphs, chapters, and exciting themes for the perfect bridge to chapter books

I Can Read Books have introduced children to the joy of reading since 1957. Featuring award-winning authors and illustrators and a fabulous cast of beloved characters, I Can Read Books set the standard for beginning readers.

A lifetime of discovery begins with the magical words **"I Can Read!"**

Visit www.icanread.com for information
on enriching your child's reading experience.

Pony Party

I Can Read Book® is a trademark of HarperCollins Publishers.

Pony Scouts: Pony Party. Copyright © 2013 by HarperCollins Publishers. All rights reserved. Manufactured in China. No part of this book may be used or reproduced in any manner without written permission except in the case of brief quotations embodied in critical articles and reviews. For information address HarperCollins Children's Books, a division of HarperCollins Publishers, 10 East 53rd Street, New York, NY 10022. www.icanread.com

Library of Congress catalog card number: 2012956501
ISBN 978-0-06-208680-8 (trade bdg.)—ISBN 978-0-06-208679-2 (pbk.)
Typography by Sean Boggs

13 14 15 16 17   SCP   10 9 8 7 6 5 4 3 2 1   ❖   First Edition

I Can Read!

READING
2
WITH HELP

PONY SCOUTS

Pony
Party

by Catherine Hapka
pictures by Anne Kennedy

HARPER
An Imprint of HarperCollinsPublishers

Jill, Meg, and Annie
were the Pony Scouts.
They loved to do anything
that involved ponies.
Today they were helping Jill's mom
run a pony party!
"I think this is the place,"
Jill's mom said.

"Hello, hello!" a woman said.

"Thanks for coming.

This is my daughter, Tina.

She's the birthday girl."

"Hi," Meg said.

"Want to watch Jill's mom

unload the ponies from the trailer?

Their names are Inky and Splash."

"No, thanks," Tina said.

Tina walked off toward the cake.

"She doesn't seem very excited,"

Jill said.

Tina's mom looked worried.

"I thought she would love

a surprise like this," she said.

"I always loved ponies

when I was her age."

"Us, too!" Meg grinned.

The Pony Scouts went to help

Jill's mom get ready.

"Who wants to go first?" Jill asked.

"The birthday girl should go first!"

Meg exclaimed.

Tina heard her and looked over.

"No, thanks," she said again.

"Someone else can go."

"Maybe she's just being polite,"

Annie whispered.

The pony rides began.

Jill's mom led Inky

while Jill led Splash.

Meg and Annie helped the kids

mount the ponies.

"I've never ridden before,"
a girl said.

"Am I doing it right?"

"You're doing great," Jill said.

"Just sit back a little more."

Soon Tina's little brother

took a turn riding Splash.

His name was Greg.

"Giddyup! I'm a cowboy!" he cried.

"How do I get this mustang to gallop?"

"Splash isn't a mustang," Jill said.

"And everyone knows real cowboys

mostly like to walk."

Soon Meg and Annie were tired

from helping the kids

into the saddle.

But they didn't mind at all.

Everyone was having fun.

Well . . . *almost* everyone.

"Tina still hasn't ridden,"

Annie whispered.

"I know," Meg said.

"What's she waiting for?"

Meg walked over to Tina.

"The ponies are waiting,"

she said with a smile.

"Which one do you want to ride?"

"Neither," Tina said with a frown.

"I don't want to get my shoes dirty."

"Whatever," Meg muttered.
She couldn't believe that Tina
cared more about clean shoes
than riding a pony!

Meg told Annie and Jill

what Tina had said.

"I think she's a snob," Meg said.

"She thinks she's too good

for us and our ponies!"

Annie looked over at Tina.

Tina was watching her brother

ride Splash around again.

"I'll be right back," Annie said.

Annie walked over to Tina.

"I already told your friend

I don't want to go on a pony ride,"

Tina said.

"Are you sure?" Annie asked.

"They're really nice and fun to ride.

But I'll tell you a secret:

I used to be afraid to ride.

Ponies are big!"

Tina didn't say anything for a second.

"Really?" she asked at last.

"You were afraid?"

"Really afraid!" Annie said.

"But I also really wanted to ride.

I was nervous the first few times.

But it was worth it."

Tina shrugged.

"Maybe I'm a tiny bit afraid, too,"

she admitted.

Annie took Tina's hand.

"Do you want to try?" she asked.

"Meg and I will stay
right beside you if you want."

"Thanks. I'd like that," Tina said.

Annie could see that Tina

was really nervous

as she climbed onto Inky's saddle.

"Ready?" Jill's mom asked.

Tina nodded. "I think so . . ."

Inky walked around

slowly in a circle.

Annie couldn't tell

if Tina was having fun.

Finally Tina dismounted.

"That was fun," she said.

"Can I try the other pony next?"

After that, Tina had a great time

at her pony party.

And so did the Pony Scouts!

PONY POINTERS

pony party: a party with ponies, of course!

trailer: a vehicle used to transport horses or ponies. A trailer is pulled behind a truck.

mounting and dismounting: getting on and off a horse or pony's back

saddle: the seat, usually made of leather, that you sit on when you ride a horse or pony